When Mommy Had a Mastectomy

When Mommy Had a Mastectomy reaches out to women and their families during an emotional and uncertain time in their lives. We are pleased and grateful to partner with INAMED Aesthetics in this book that addresses such a critical issue for women faced with breast surgery following cancer.

With less than half of mastectomy patients seeking reconstruction, the need for education and awareness in this area is essential. INAMED Aesthetics is committed to helping women become more informed about breast cancer treatment and their options for reconstruction. We appreciate their recognition that this book will help encourage discussion between mothers and their children, and thus alleviate some of the fear associated with breast surgery.

INAMED Aesthetics's commitment to restoring the lives of breast cancer patients through innovative breast reconstruction products helps women restore wholeness and complete the healing process.

A portion of the proceeds of the sale of this book will be donated to the Y-ME National Breast Cancer Organization and the Susan B. Komen Foundation.

When Mommy Had a Mastectomy

Nancy Reuben Greenfield

Illustrated by Ralph Butler

Bartleby Press
Silver Spring, Maryland

Thanks to God for my blessings; to all my friends and family for nurturing me through my breast cancer; to Wendy Harpham, M.D. for her excellent edits on my manuscript; and to Dianne Martin and INAMED for their generous commitment to making my book available to so many who need it. —NRG

Printed in China

Bartleby Press
PO Box 1516
Silver Spring, Maryland 20915
800-953-9929
www.BartlebythePublisher.com

Library of Congress Cataloging-in-Publication Data

Greenfield, Nancy Reuben.
When mommy had a mastectomy / Nancy Reuben Greenfield ; illustrated by Ralph Butler.
p. cm.
ISBN 0-910155-60-7
1. Mastectomy--Juvenile literature. 2. Breast--Cancer--Surgery--Juvenile literature. 3. Surgery, Plastic--Juvenile literature. 4. Breast--Cancer--Patients--Family relationships--Juvenile literature. I. Butler, Ralph M. II. Title.

RD667.5.G745 2004
616.99'449059--dc22
2004020757

With love to my husband, Richard,
and our two compassionate children,
Joshua and Gabrielle

There's nothing I like better...

eating ice cream

swinging

...than hugging
my mommy.

We have a special hug,
Mommy and I, where I lay my
head upon her chest, my face
resting upon her breasts.

That changed the day Mommy told me she had cancer in her breast. This breast cancer meant Mommy must go to the hospital to have an operation called a mastectomy to remove her breast and the cancer in it. The operation, she told me, would make her feel sick and take a while to heal.

After she said
this, we were
sad together.

Then Mommy held my hands and told me cancer wasn't like a cold. I couldn't catch her cancer. And nothing, absolutely nothing, I did or even thought about doing caused her cancer.

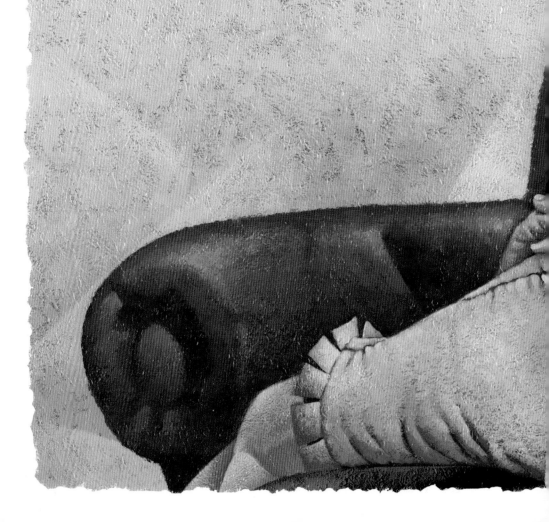

Mommy didn't know why she got breast cancer but she did know this operation, called a mastectomy, would help her live longer.

I was worried about how Mommy would look without a breast. Mommy said she had thought about that too. Women with breast cancer have a choice about how they look after a mastectomy.

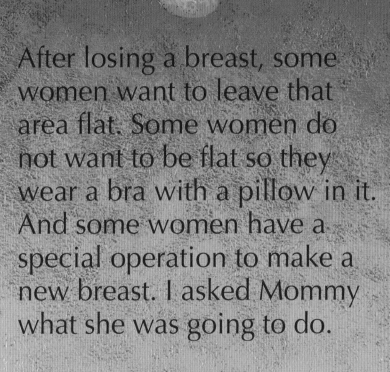

After losing a breast, some women want to leave that area flat. Some women do not want to be flat so they wear a bra with a pillow in it. And some women have a special operation to make a new breast. I asked Mommy what she was going to do.

She said she was going to have the special operation to make a new breast but this time wanted it filled up with chocolate milk! We both laughed. Oh, how we wish she could.

It was hard to say "goodbye" before
Mommy went to the hospital. I was afraid I
would never talk to her or see her again,
but I did. At first, we spoke over the phone.

Later, I visited Mommy in the hospital. She looked so sick. I was glad nurses and doctors were taking such good care of her.

After a few days, Mommy came home. She was in a lot of pain and it was hard for me to see Mommy hurting.

I tried to help
Mommy feel
better in my
special
ways...

dressing myself...

It seemed like forever that my Mommy was sick and needed to rest. Even when she was up, she didn't feel like playing or sometimes even talking.

I missed the way it used to be with Mommy. The worst part, though, was not being able to do our special hug.

So we learned to hug in other ways!

hugging hands

hugging toes

hugging out loud

hugging elbows

cooking...

going grocery shopping...

It took a long time before Mommy was doing all the things mommies do...

driving the car...

I was thankful that my mommy was feeling better.

tucking me in bed at night.

Then one day...

One wonderful day...

My mommy brought my head
ever so gently to her chest,
my face resting softly
upon her new breast.

It was our special hug
as sweet as it could be!
Now all our hugs are
so much more special for me.

There is nothing I like better than hugging my Mommy.